Buffalo
Dust

Buffalo Dust

Photo: Len Kagelmacher

Poems by
George T. Hole

Buffalo Arts Publishing

Buffalo Dust. Copyright © 2017 by George T. Hole. Printed in the United States of America. All rights reserved. No part of this book may be reproduced or transmitted in any form or by any means without written permission of the author. For information, address Buffalo Arts Publishing, 179 Greenfield Drive, Tonawanda, NY 14150

Email: info@buffaloartspublishing.com

Cover design by Len Kagelmacher

ISBN 978-0-9978741-1-2

Dedicated to

John Carbonara

Acknowledgements

The following poems in this book have been previously published:

"Wind Storm | Ice Storm" *Both Sides Now* (Earth's Daughters, #81, 2013.)
"Three Incarnations of a Fly" *Sugar Mule*, November 2008.
"Shoelace Sutra" *Sugar Mule*, November 2008.
"Lackawanna Mills" *Buffalo News*, Sunday, July 6, 2008.
"Watermelon from the Original Garden" *Buffalo News*, Sunday, January 2, 2005.
"In Gauguin's Painting It Watches a Reclining Nude" *Stone Drum*, vol. 9, #3.

For their support to WNY poets and poetry, special thanks to

Barbara Hole
Robert Pohl
ryki zuckerman

and to

Lin Xia Jiang for his portrait on the last page
and Len Kagelmacher for his photography

Contents

Over the Skyway

    Lackawanna Mills 11
    Side-View Mirror 12
    The Shoelace Sutra 13
    Two Kinds of Paintings 14
    Wind Storm | Ice Storm 15
    In Gauguin's Painting
        It Watches a Reclining Nude 16
    If he did not paint lying on his back,
        as the story goes 17
    While Posing for My Portrait 19
    Watermelon from the Original Garden 21
    Whispers 23
    The Love of Three Oranges 24

Red Jacket

    Three Incarnations of a Fly 27
    Angry He Was 28
    Why Man, Why 30
    Achilles 31
    After Hours 33
    Crows 34
    Defending the Homeland 36
    Red Jacket 38
    Four-Faced Buddha 41

Buffalo Dust

    Dust 43
    For jcjc 46
    My soul to take 48

About the Poet 50

Over the Skyway

Photo: Len Kagelmacher

Lackawanna Mills

Driving out of Buffalo over the Skyway
Into Lackawanna you used to be able to see
The night sky on fire, then smell the acid air
From blast furnaces molding I-beams and hope.
The mills starved, closed, rusted and became scrap
As did the workers who drank salted water and
Said their daily prayers at the edge of hell-hot glory holes.
Old-timers tell stories about steel and bankruptcy
And nurse what beer they can afford on their promise-broken pensions.
They are not Christ's salt-of-the-earth or slag.
They watch TV all night with no sound on.
Listen to police sirens. Some phone
800-number girls for a reminder of sex.
Some repent. Some protest to parish priests.

New giants pierce the sky where mills once were:
—Look beyond the weeds and boxcars rusted onto rail tracks—
Eight silver ballerinas have reincarnated as wind turbines.
They rise above Lake Erie in shocking grace.
On clear nights the turbine blades send stars dancing
Across ground and water, like be-jeweled dervishes.
Tchaikovsky heard rumors of them in the underworld.
He is composing a new Swan Lake for them.
Tai Chi masters in China imitate their move-hands-like-clouds meditation.
Cervantes wrote an epilogue: Don Quixote will gallop
Across the Atlantic on his nag to battle these new-fangled windmills.
Supposedly mad, at first sight of them, kneel, he must.
Lose memory of war-oaths. Listen to their whirling love moans.
So, it must be possible to imagine
Bodies born in the manger of Bethlehem Corp
Breaking out of their steel cocoons.

Side-View Mirror

In moon-time it must have spun
Its dew-dropped web in this most improbable place.
One thread is anchored to my driver-side mirror
The other two are anchored, for the moment,
Between door and closed door-window.
As I race the speed limit I witness
Web-destruction. Stupid spider,
Except it reappears the next morning,
The web again lacing emptiness into a delicate trap.

Day after day I am the whirlwind god
Devoted to road-webs with dangerous intersections
And landscapes of nothing but arrival.
The radio announces the last aria of Pavarotti.
Later voices discuss the discovery of the largest space
Of absolute nothing in the universe.
In the mirror I see what might dare pass me
And see the spider who hangs on, spinning
Like a cyclone at the end of its last thread.

For sure I end this one-sided courtship
As I wash the car with a requiem-tuned hose.
I avoid spraying the mirror home
Where my spider hides. Desperate
It must be, for company, to reappear
In my race-world existence unless
It has a lover's design on me
As its most rare and delicious prey.
The next day I ride spider-free.

The next morning I discover frost on the grass
And there, on the back of my car
In the bike rack, is a glistening new web.
I let my breath touch it. With this hitch-hiking
Omen I will drive into winter.

The Shoelace Sutra

All right Buddha, this is not one
Of your Sanskrit scriptures
Translated letter by letter for centuries
By nameless monks. No, it is my silent broadcast
As I compose myself with numberless breaths.
On a black cushion I sit in hope
Of grasping enlightenment, though I confess
I only know what books say it is.
The incense burns.
The moment is, well, just the moment.

My eyes fix on my running shoes
Like two relatives come home, lots older,
Ready to tell stories about a world where
Paths lie open for boundless running.
(Most compassionate Buddha, please
Add a sign in your Eightfold Path for old jocks.)
Those shoe laces, so graceful. They gesture:
Here there are no knots to suffer untying.
My knees crave unbending.
Body cries for release.

I vanish into those perfectly-sized empty foot-spaces.
Would trade enlightenment for one more run,
Glorious, of course. But the thought dissolved
In oblivion. I recover myself
Back on the cushion itching.
I complain about the gravity of always being in
Just-this present-moment. My devoted
Running shoes want to be immediately laced.
Incense burns, as do desires.
My mind runs crazy.

Two Kinds of Paintings

Imagine, the rock shore, eroded banks
And nude trees of Evangola State Park
Plastered, as if by a mad wall-papering dervish,
With reddish-orange and blacks, using lots of glue
To hold tens of thousands of monarch
Butterflies, everywhere, on rocks, on trees.
Weary ones riding the thin surface tension of water.
The wind flutters their exhausted wings.
They have crossed Lake Erie and temptation
To be knelt down in this place, before they must
Rise again to find for the first time their nectar-home
In Mexico. After mating they fly North again
Following the sun and the lure of milkweed,
Living no longer than one circuit of the moon.
Will a another generation of chrysalis-awaken children
Transfigured with wings find this Lake edge again,
And the good fortune of a tail-wind crossing?

The eyes in Burchfield's painting *Wind-blown Asters*
Are almost blown off the canvas, as are other
Flower-eyes with their eyelashes verging on
Amazement. Everything alive above soil arches
Backward from Heraclitus' pulse of fiery-desire
And shimmers with the touch of salvation. Almost
Disguised two butterfly wings do not waver, do not feel doubt
As do the worms and other eyeless dirt eaters
Below who share dark-matter with the buried dead.

Wind Storm | Ice Storm

In Charles Burchfield's paintings winds shake clouds,
Breaking them through a prism of imagination
So their edges vibrate colors.
His wind is so full of its almighty self that trees
Bow to its straight-ahead desire and grass too
All bend like fragile ballerinas,
So even worms in the underworld pause
Wondering what awful wish,
Unfulfilled, rubs up and down their soft skin.

Unfulfilled like fear, the face of this
October storm-night is masked in clear crystal.
Crack. So like a rifle shot. I ducked. Another
Crack another target cries out.
Surrounded, I must have stepped into a war
With invisible snipers too insane
To shoot straight. Everywhere tree branches
Fall down dead-drunk, while
More ice so glazes trees and ground they
Fail to recognize themselves. Fallen wires
Whip the ground speaking in bursts of orange tongue.
With a rake handle I free low branches
Held captive in perfectly fitting ice-skin.

Too late to save anything closer to heaven.
For these amputated trees I pray
To what good-god who pushed creation's pulse
As if in rage, pushed to rupture point.
Then curse. Breath undergoes a conversion to ice particles.

In Gauguin's Painting
It Watches a Reclining Nude

—at Albright-Knox, waiting to see you

looking
there in the mirror

of loneliness
behind the face

the hollows dilating
the

other eyes
the Spirit of Death watching

itself
it seems

asking
if only

you were not
so faithful a lover

if only you would
help me

conclude this
this

If he did not paint lying on his back, as the story goes

Michael the earth-bound angel
Created God's and Adam's
Fingers so close before the shock
Of the double awaking,
Adam to his father and God
Awaking to his first-born son.

First, Michelangelo drew on paper
A figure, poked holes into it, pressed it
Against the ceiling, shot soot
Though the holes to outline
The body of God, like the lines
In a child's coloring book.

He reached out with his brush,
His hand dyed with sky blue
The brush a lightning rod
Trembling as he reached
For God's finger to let fall
One last caress of paint.

What work do the priests do,
Black ants, back-bent,
Carrying their daily trespasses
Under his scaffold
Under the weight
Of their whispering rosary beads?

It was not Plato's ladder of love
Michael climbed up and down for four years.
Not painting for heaven's sake. Not for El Papa.
His workers climbed for neither,
Climbed with their loaves
And fishes of plaster for a few lira.

Did Adam hear God coming?
See what awe pointed at him alone?
Did he wonder about the dream—
Look there on his thigh—
The dream hiding in his limp penis?
Did he wonder about consequences?

In the shadow show of candle light
Michael watched the sleepless flight
Of angel wings crisscrossing his ceiling.
On nights blinded from plaster dust
Mixed with lime and paint, he felt flying
Demons set free from the Book of Revelations.

In the winter he shivered in
His Sistine heaven. At siesta
He stared at his Adam,
Remembered not to drink too much
Wine with his loaf of bread and olives.
The fall to the floor would be easy.

On Michael's Last Judgment the pope ordered
The genitals of Jesus painted over.
His brushes are caked dry. He lays down
Where imagination must fail. He dreams
His finger is Adam's ready
For the shock of a second life.

While Posing for a Portrait

—for Lin Xia Jiang: Artist, Teacher, Friend

1.
Try not to move.
I try, without hammer, mallet and chisel,
To sculpt myself exactly into my own body space.

Stop. I interrupt my muttering to almost shout
To my twitching face muscles, stop,
Or like Humpty-Dumpty I will shatter.

2.
I see only the blank side
Of canvas, not knowing
What semblance of me
Will emerge out of white nothing.

Plato snickers. As both the model and image
He tells me I glimmer
Only as two second-hand shadows.

3.
Eye floaters are
Thousands of newly born spiders,
Air-borne, on the ends of silver threads,
With no thoughts of earth landing,
No blue-prints for web-building, and
No appetite for fly-blood.

I reappear inside my arm
Draped over the decrepit blue couch,
Where needles are dancing the tarantella.

4.
I pretend to be Leonardo with his brush
Soaked in pigments suspended in oil,
About to caress Mona Lisa's lips.
What did he feel?

Behind bullet proof glass, safe
From millions of touring eyes crawling
Like ants over her face
Hungry for a taste of forbidden fruit,
What does she feel?

Watermelon from the Original Garden

—for my daughter Lauren Lynn

20% chance of thunder showers, says the weatherman
Cheerfully. He disappears as the screen answers
Our daily hopes with maps and numbers, like dew point
35°C, which, I doubt, few of us understand.
For news of hurricanes, blizzards, floods his voice deepens
To eulogy and he gives us more facts than usual
To save our imaginations from the weather outside.
Doctors are not much different.

What do I make of the facts? Wilm's tumor. Stage IV.
Seems like a choice film. Great drama, >65% survival
Rate after 5 years. But, depends on the cell type.
How do we exit a bad movie? I remember
You, at two, in your watermelon night-shirt,
Sweeter by far, pits and all, sweeter than
Watermelon from the original garden. The news is
Reddish-pink, as in flesh; is pits, as
In innocent flaws, growing inside, as in
Cancer. They cut it out, drugged
It out, burned it out; they said. Thank
God they left me you.

What do I make of the odds? I pace,
A zoo cat, pace having the luxury of
Connecting cages. From kitchen, to dining room,
Past front door, to living room, past front door,
Other way into kitchen (sometimes detouring
Through sunroom into backyard and back into kitchen) and
Around again, carrying you. We say little
Out loud. Your skin burns from radiation. I try
To send you magic. Try carrying the odds.

No 65% of you can survive. Try carrying all or
Nothing of you. No odds. No facts. Lost,
Between rooms, between treatments and nausea, no maps.
You send me your magic. Desperate love is the best we can do.

Your hair has grown back. We rarely speak of that time.
We speak in usual ways. You have learned to say *Like*
And *You know*; and I learned *Did you?* and *No*.
Did you send a thank you note? I ask again. *Yes*,
You say in all your blue-eyed radiance. *Did you*
Mail it, I ask. *No*, you say. So I speak the way
Parents are supposed to. Pay attention. So I say *Thank you*
For asking 'How was your day, Dad.' Thank you for
Interrupting my work with a homework problem. Thank you
For letting me pace with you around the kitchen looking
For snacks after school, looking for a special title
For your assignment, a poem, about your essence.
Watermelon. *Yes*, we say. *Yes*, thank you for your life.

Whispers

Whispers waiting in the sheets
Cover and comfort us
In our near-touching. Day-flushed
We fall into separate sleeps.

A dreamer goes underwater.
The bottom. Where is it?
Your hand? Hell-No I shout myself to awake.
In first light we join empty hand to empty hand

Then, taking turns, one go down stairs,
Lets the dogs out into the backyard,
(to relieve themselves and bark until fed)
And mounting the carpeted stairs, one will return

With black coffee for both our thirsts.
We must step out of our pajamas, two
Chaste mannequins, and step into ourselves and
Next step into the world. We leave behind

On the back of the bathroom door
Our pajamas hanging empty of form and flesh.
They hope for the return of our bodies
And their dreams of desire.

The Love of Three Oranges

—an opera by Prokofiev

I heard the title and later
Read the story of the melancholic
Prince who was cursed to love and
Had to find three magic oranges. No surprise,
The first two he found and cut open
Ended badly. The last revealed a princess
His instantaneous love, aroused, to last forever. Except,
Love was interrupted when she,
His one-and-only orange, his Princess
Resurrected, was once again revised
By another jealous witch, became a giant rat.

Love, on stage, love, I ought to know,
Like death, absurdly triumphs in the end.
I had originally supposed, the three oranges,
Yes, the oranges were in love with each other.
I heard the title, like gossip,
And was excited by what I imagined.

Screw the plot. Imagine for a moment three oranges,
Ordinary except they are in love. With each other.
See them, two perfectly oval orange breasts
Or two balls aching for love. Bashful
The third hides from lecherous eyes. They are
Recklessly alive, not languishing on a blue plate
With grapes and a brown banana, forsaken
By the obscure painter who fell in love
With a copy of them on white canvas.

They even survived Picasso's surgery, being sliced into cubes.
So alive, they live beyond incarnation and the rot of saints.
Sense their insides swelling. Their musky desire would make sin
Glisten, in a garden where weeds, bugs, bad weather,
And tempting snakes all blossom together, heedless
Of any order, human or divine. Like surprise flowers
From Anonymous, they appear on your dining room table
Set with your best China, linen napkins,
And a clear glass bowl in the center, set for
A dinner party for friends. There they are, three oranges in love,
Uninvited guests, who are happy to perform, at long last,
Prokofiev's lost aria, of ecstatic sex.

Red Jacket

Photo: Public Domain

Three Incarnations of a Fly

1. Evil in the kitchen

The fly, unknown to itself—an instance
Of family Muscidae—feels the air rush-by
Flits and alights elsewhere, again and again, effortlessly.
A mind, unknown to itself as billions of blinking neurons,
Follows that fly, knowing evil in the kitchen.
The hand, swat-drunken and failing its pure mind,
Flails the swatter
And misses again and again,
Is fueled by curses,
Is desperate, hiding from emptiness,
Is human in the hope of killing.
After satisfaction a small mess will need
Strong water and a scrubbing hand.

2. Not form, not emptiness

Her two soggy housefly-wings fight against each other
Flail against the unknown stickiness
Of foreign tongue. Yet, in a Buddha moment of realization,
The taste buds in her feet taste something strange, tasting like herself.
Not yet, before the lizard-swallow, a question sounds.
Wake up. Wake.

3. Enlightenment

Quick tongue-snap in-curl, the fly—
Who lives off sweet rotting fruit—
Takes the form of lizard mouth and begins
A selfless journey into an asylum of juices.

Angry He Was

> —Delaware Lake near the Casino

Angry he was as only a father can *God-damn*,
Forgetting his own double-dares leaps,
As a police diver appeared from under black water
With the weed-tangled body of his son.

A stranger pumps on his boy's chest,
Repeats anxious numbers, brings up
Only water and white-thick drool.
Then a body-spasm. A second miraculous one.

It was not like when, at age five, I watched
My volunteer-fireman father float to shore
A bloated body, chained to his boat,
With grappling hooks. *He's one dead fish* someone joked.

He's alive leap-frogged through the crowd
Right before the boy was pronounced dead.
God damn him the father cursed again, kicked
The zipped-up black bag, the corpse inside.

I did not confess what I could not do.
From picnic table and book, I had come
To the high-banked water's edge, minutes after
I heard the electric rumor, a boy has drowned.

No guardian angel, I stood dry
Above two boys who screamed,
Gasped for air and dove underwater again
Into coffin-dark to find their sunken friend.

His jeans and sweatshirt were black I was told.
His skin was black, too. Without oxygen
For so long, even if his heart still beat, I thought
Water-logged wires would unplug his brain.

So, I was ready to save, only if necessary,
His two friends, breaking free
Of deep-water's grip, gulping air, and
Diving into despair again and again.

In dream I surrender to the gravity of no excuses,
Surrender to a black-body hanging heavy on me
Who kneels me in slime and weed bottom, in front of
An entrance sign: *Hell, for Whites Only*.

Why Man, Why

Man, you must be brain-dead dumb
To ask me why I done what I done.
Don't go blame my God-sick mother
Or put on the news my shit-faced father.

Just for fun ask my teacher to explain
Why do I have to add numbers with a's and b's
To guess what stupid x supposed to be equal to?

What equals these warm-dead kids on the floor?
Cause, they don't F-ing know what is x either.
Crack open my skull. Do whatever you need to do.
Just don't ask me nothing no more.

Man, you must be dumb and blind.
Can't you see the hole in my dumb-ass head
And, cradled in my hell-bound hand, the guilty-empty gun?

Achilles

Headline Achilles
Killed proved wrong.
He was choppered
To a trauma unit.
Said nothing when he saw
The space where
His foot should have been.

The ward was a gimp nest
Without feathers where
On schedule nurses
Dropped pills into beaks
Chirping for more.
Lucky for booze and drugs
Smuggled in.
Not for Achilles.
Rehab was wrath of the gods
For warriors kneed in the balls
For following presidential orders.

News chatter. Achilles
Was healing, has cash
Promised for his name
On a cereal box and video game
Just more humiliations
He was fighting against.
Aroused, being again
Honor-avenging Achilles
Did return to war
When he found the last
Of his platoon-brothers were
Waiting in line outside the VA
Like sinners waiting
At the gates of hell.
He ascended in his chair with shinny wheels

To the plush top of their Washington bunker,
Chased down the administration gods.
Took honorable testimony with a hot AK-47.
Mission done, he made peace
With his loyal 45. Evening
Headline GNP Improves.

Oh, Goddess,
Missing in action,
There are so many far flung wars
To fight or pout about.
Wake the dead:
Inspire Homer to write a sequel
About our Achilles.
Implore Exekias
To paint an amphora
Of him, like the one
Behind bullet-proof
Glass in the Vatican.
Instruct lame Hephaestus:
To make a new shield
Emblazoned with noble images
For our soldiers. None were dipped in
A river of immortality.

After Hours

    —where AM&A's used to be on Sheridan

The perfectly laid-out parking lot,
Must know this is the last-minute descent into closing time.

In windows, manikins promise to always smile as they will pose
Throughout another night without orgasm.

Only a few metal auto-beasts wait dutifully
For their drive-masters to return. And they do.

Empty hands going in emerge holding bag. Exit-eyes hurry
To fix a direction; ignition keys click for

Head-lights to wink back; unlocked, the safe-insides light up.
What remains? The very last hands went inside the store full

And returned empty. Workers scatter home. Far into the night
The white parking lines, tire-stained, still on duty, dare not wish

To break geometry and touch one another, across the empty space.
One beast, a new model, waits, as if in meditation.

No secret lovers steam the inside.
It does not hear any footsteps approaching.

From their towers bold lights blot out the stars
And keep watch over everything below.

Crows

Tethered to a steel pole holding
Tubes of medicine and a monitor for vital-signs
I look out the 7th floor Millard Fillmore window
And watch crows fly by, like drunks
Staggering toward just one more drink,
Hundreds of them, each damn one
An aerial cross—an empty crucifix, minus an omen
Or obscenity, only blank blackboards.
Where they roost they will speak in insults
And joust for the best limb to dream on.

Strange warriors they are. Even alone,
They are known to attack hawks,
Despite the odds of going against talons and beak.
But they lurch like a heavy bomber
Under attack by a squadron of sparrows.
At daybreak they will abandon Riverside Park
(Where homeless men sleep under their trees)
And zigzag to a faraway field for feed and solitude.

At twelve, proud of a new shotgun,
To perfect my aim and steady squeeze,
I used crows for easy target practice. It
Was easy. I left Auburn New York, my hunting-home,
Christened from a poem line, *Sweet Auburn!*
Loveliest village of the plain and its lovely
Penitentiary-home with the first chair for
Electrocutions. Left home,
To study laws of physics.

Every night at dusk, National Geographic reported,
Upwards of 50,000 crows
(Double the number of people still in Auburn)
Nervously descend on Fort Hill Cemetery.
It did not report they
Drop their wet white-shit on the dead.

Not a sin, like the clot
Damming an artery in my head. An occlusion
Doctors named it and are able to do
Nothing else. It waits, ready, any day,
By pure chance, to burst my brain

So I will end, a clump on the ground, just
Like a pellet-riddled crow staring
At nowhere with an unblinking eye.

I push my pole back to my room,
Push crows out of mind,
Push quickly past open doors
Exposing white sheets caressing
Wounded bodies, the lucky ones
Soothed by family or uniforms,
Grey green for doctors, white for nurses.
Most rooms are sealed from view.

The man I share a room with whose brain
Is more clogged or more empty than mine,
Sleeps all day. At crow time
He will sit on the edge of his bed and piss on the floor
As a glimmer of him stammers for revenge.
He will seem to watch television all the high-volume night.
I press the nurse button so she will pull
The curtain closed, creating a backlit screen
On which I watch silhouettes cross back and silently forth,
Like ghosts of remorseless crows, like drones
Waiting for the divine order to break the dimension of sky
To complete their mission.

Defending the Homeland

> "war is premised upon deception, motivated by advantage"
> —*The Art of War*

In the beginning of sword time
Master Sun warned serious warriors
That warfare is the great affair of life and death,
The way of preservation and extinction.
To defend the homeland I know how
Easy it is to wipe out ground troops

Of ants marching in line under heavy food packs.
Easy to put a heel to them or, better, follow them
To their humpback home, a slum of tunnels,
And crush it and all of them with a foot-stamping dance.
Though I learned to be ready, ants will have their dance
Of revenge when they crawl up my legs

And inside the clothes of lovers lying in the grass.
Easy against other bug-vators to use the same squashing
Fate, even for night-stealing mice.
Set with care the spring to snap
A neck not a warrior's finger. My advice:
Keep family protestors silent, especially the kids,

By secretly disposing their small asleep-like bodies.
Sacrifice any shine of glory—one
Of many hardships of a warrior's life.
Airborne enemies need sophisticated weapons.
In the old days, through friendly summer windows,
Flies would launch their buzz attacks, evading swatter

And curses. Now, with the closing of windows
To save the air conditioning, the fly trap, the long

Twisting band of sticky stuff, hanging from the ceiling
Like crepe left over from a party, was made extinct
By the spray can, ideal for a perfumed kill.
But outside in backyard jungles the orange candles

And spray-on armor hardly protect against
The needle-stick and suck of mosquitos and after-itching.
The bee, thank goodness, has no passion for war,
Except the mad wasp when high up a ladder,
Under a rafter its mad house is disturbed.
Though the honey bee might be

Conspiring inside the ear of flowers.
Worse than the clumsy bee is the rogue bat
Circling the bedroom ceiling in a halo
Radiating signals from hell to wake a soul half-alive.
But, what enemies unknown wait,
Happy in hate in the homeland?

Rumors infected news: Our drinking water crawls with invisible
Agents. Are worms secret weapons? Wake up Master Sun.
I do not own a sword. Kitchen knives will not do.
Where can I order on-line a tank and a drone
The size of a mosquito for spying on my foreign neighbor
And a dutiful drone carrying a big-enough bomb.

Red Jacket

"You have now become a great people, and we have scarcely a place left to spread our blankets. You have got our country, but are not satisfied; you want to force your religion upon us".
—From his speech to the U.S. Senate, 1805.

He got bored being just
A statue, unpaid as an unarmed
Sentinel at the entrance to a cemetery
Where dogs are forbidden
And most visitors are runners,
Even in snow. Crows fly in at sunset,
Coughing like patients in a TB sanitarium.
They drop their white ooze to
Stake a claim on whatever riches
Lie below. The dead don't care.
At least the White folks buried there
Don't, (included are a few Blacks.)
The Red ones lie scattered around Buffalo
In unknown burial grounds built
And paved over. Easier to find
An arrowhead in the back yard. Curious,
Red Jacket climbs off his high stone-slab

He heard rumors from visitors
Of the dead about Tonto
Talking Kemo Sabe to the Lone Ranger.
About Jim Thorpe's records.
About the exclusive Buffalo
Club serving bison burgers.
To check, Red Jacket goes
In search of the Seneca Casino
Somewhere past left-over
Mansions on Delaware Ave.
It's not a long walk unless you are
Arthritic from posing
Motionless for countless moons.

He wonders, is the Great Spirit
There? Are his brothers still
Thought of as savages?
Are they still in the business
Of bartering themselves for White man's
Drink? He doesn't know, walking the street,
He could be arrested for
Being homeless or dressing
Almost like an Indian.
He wonders will the cemetery be
Left unguarded; remembers
How the traffic turns dangerous when
The suburbs enter and exit the city
Except on Thanksgiving Day when
Delaware is blocked off
For the Turkey Trot race.
Some of the 25,000 runners
Dress as Indians.

Is anyone looking for him,
Alias Sa-Go-Ye-Wat-Ha?
Branded "t-rex killer"
For maybe murdering a cow.
As a wanted poster
One his many portraits will do:
He always wears something red.

On the front-face of his jacket,
A large solid-silver glob hangs
From his neck, the "Peace Medal"
Given him by President Washington.
Dangerous, in all his portraits,
He cradles a scalping hatchet.

Thus far, there have been
No wanted-person sightings.
Is it possible he found out
The smoke in the casino
Is worse than teepee smoke?
So, is he headed elsewhere?
Following what remains
Of old trails to Washington
To negotiate a new treaty?
Or, go on the war path?

Four-Faced Buddha

In Beijng, in a street of ominous antique shops
I bargained for a small four-faced Buddha.
Cast from bronze, so the seller said.
Like a compass, I believed, each face fixed a direction,
So no matter which way I turned
The needle would point me toward enlightenment.

By the front door on a wainscot ledge Buddha
Meditates, where a fall would, like ambition,
Have consequences. Better it would be,
I have heard, to fall into a manure pile
To stay in it like a guest and feel
Its heat fertilize one's soul.

Mornings, after I glance
In the mirror and sigh
I twist Buddha to
Fix my moods for the sake of
Wife kids dogs and unsuspecting world
—and choose one of his faces to wear.

All cars stop. Ahead an accident?
Horns curse. Nowhere to hurry to.
Alone in my car, the roof a Bodhi tree,
Buddha and radio remind me
Suffering is like air and
Also like its absence.

Not counting breaths. My mother's voice
Returns from the dead: Always stick to
How you were brought up. Meaning, stop complaining.
Bear your cross of original sin. Compassionate one,
Save me from the desire for the apple forever
Dangling on the tree in that foolish garden.

Buffalo Dust

Photo: Len Kagelmacher

Dust

<u>Noun</u>
According to the place where words
Stand at attention, in a line up,
Exposing their rap-sheet,
Dust is
A fine, dry powder consisting
Of tiny particles of earth
Or waste matter carried in air
Or lying on the ground or on surfaces.
According to a solemn place
Put forth as an example
In a high-strutting sentence,
Dust is
Dust thou art. But
What kind of dust?
Plain dirt-dust or gold dust?
Saw or fairy? Dust
In road dust? Dust storm? Dust
Devil? Dust Bowl?

<u>Interrogative</u>
What kind of sentence?
Bite the dust. Who?
Throw dust. Where?
In God's eye. Adam run!
Leave in dust. Why?

<u>Verb</u>
To dust, to spiff up.
To be free, perfectly dust-free,
According to the Queen of Unclutter,
Just hug all your belongings, see
If they spark joy. If not
Toss them out, then
Dust off your hands

Dust them with sprinkles of sugar.
Failing to dust leaves a print
Of an idle soul, such as
A man living alone in shelves of books
Naked without their jackets
Waiting motionless in line
While the dust grows literate,
Such as an old woman, usually widowed,
Or a wife in the afternoon whose
House coat collects
Dust all by itself.

Present Participle
Dust-fall on window
In glass, moon and face look back.
Shadows waits off-stage.

Slang
Dust off, as in
A pitch, inside and head-high
Warning the batter.
For crime talk and gang talk
Dust off, as in kill, as in knock
Off, or eliminating a syllable,
Simply as off the bastard.

Past Tense*
Called scoopers. They worked
In dust. Their sweat mixed with wheat
In cement cylinders known as grain elevators.
Out of the bellies of lake freighters,
The golden kernels shook free
Of husks and seeds
Were sucked in big straws
To the tops of those hungry giants
So gravity could fed them on command
Down into bags for truck-loading. Men

At the bottom worked in what spilled over.
Hard work. Hard breaths. They were
Brothers to miners with black lungs
Breath-short even on the level.
They joked that the final product
Was not Cheerios
Destined for the breakfast bowl
But whiskey fermenting in their bottle
Of air, dripping down their foreheads
To lips, onto lips. Bonus pay.
They were a choir of shovels. Were
Wheat dust, mixed with rat dust
Mixed with one stray motor-spark.
Became dust imperceptibly
Muddled in dust.

*Buffalo, June 25. 1913 -- According to the estimate made this afternoon by police, twenty-six of the men employed in the mill when it was blown up by an explosion yesterday afternoon are still unaccounted for. *Olean Times*

For jcjc

   1935—2016

I was reading the last installment
Of your journal about how
In the Navy you floated over
The sunken homes of brother sailors
But never spoke to them, seaman to seaman,
When you had the chance.
Your version of sin.
I wrote a quick something,
Hit send expecting
Your usual after-midnight message.

After your funeral
Your wife told me
After serving coffee
And left-over memorial muffins
How you left
The faucet on
When you fell to
The bathroom floor,
Stubbornly dead.
She repeated all the details.
So, about the time I hit send
Emergency guys were giving
You breaths and chest push-downs
You could not answer.

In your attic we paused
As I offered a few poor compliments
About her gallery of water-colors
Then passed for the first time into your hermitage
Where I know your soul only spoke to itself

At exactly the place you used
As your pseudonym-signature
    Lat 42.54 N
    Long 78.51 W
Together with your
Initials mysteriously doubled.

We were in search of the password to your computer
—a surprise, there were six of them with connecting wires
Dangling nowhere special off the shelf—
Not likely you wrote the secret
Word down in an obvious hiding place
In case of memory loss or worse.
None the less we looked in hope to kick start
The light-speed dance of 1's and 0's
Immobilized in that small black vault
That held mute more writings
You were emailing me in spurts.

In this fragile hereafter
Waiting with cold coffee
At Denny's on Delaware
A space we knew by heart.
I ignore the waitress'
Request for my order
As I ignored an answer to
Your latest request that
I would become your brother.

My soul to take

She would have
Kissed you goodnight
And reminded, *Say your prayers*.
But, you rolled over
Faced the wall
Made-believe you were
Lost in sleep.
Hiding what?

What had Mother done?
Give little brother
The bigger half?
Made fun giving you a bath?
Scream out
Your fist-clenched words
Or let loose
That frightful need.

Why did you choose instead
A lullaby of pillow,
Your arms bear-hugging it,
Face buried,
Reciting *If I should die*
While imagining what happens
Below in the cellar where
Chickens lose their heads
For Sunday dinners.

What offense? I don't remember.
Besides she's dead.
Others have taken her place.
If I could find where he hides
I would hold and kiss

That wall-turned boy
Then, I pray my soul to take
Back, I would smack him.
Stop squandering our life.

About the Poet

Portrait by Lin Xia Jiang

George T. Hole graduated from the University of Rochester with a B.A in physics and a Ph.D. in Philosophy. He was inducted into the University Sports Hall of Fame for his record performances in football and track. He retired from Buffalo State College as SUNY Distinguished Teaching Professor of Philosophy. His poems have been published in *Cimmaron Review*, *Rapport*, *Stone Drum*, *Earth's Daughters*, and *Sugar Mule*, as well as *The Buffalo News*. He is the author of Thinking Well about What Matters and philosophy essays on Socrates, films and counseling.

For more information about George Hole, visit
http://philosophy.buffalostate.edu/george-hole

www.ingramcontent.com/pod-product-compliance
Lightning Source LLC
Chambersburg PA
CBHW040336300426
44113CB00021B/2765